MURRAY AVE. L
LOWER MORELAND S
HUNTINGDON VLY., PA.

DIRT BIKES

Sarah Tieck

Big Buddy BOOKS
Amazing Vehicles

ABDO
Publishing Company

Amazing Vehicles

VISIT US AT
www.abdopublishing.com

Published by ABDO Publishing Company, 8000 West 78th Street, Edina, Minnesota 55439.

Copyright © 2010 by Abdo Consulting Group, Inc. International copyrights reserved in all countries. No part of this book may be reproduced in any form without written permission from the publisher. Buddy Books™ is a trademark and logo of ABDO Publishing Company.

Printed in the United States.

Coordinating Series Editor: Rochelle Baltzer
Contributing Editors: Megan M. Gunderson, BreAnn Rumsch, Marcia Zappa
Graphic Design: Deb Coldiron, Marcia Zappa
Cover Photograph: *iStockphoto.com*: ©iStockphoto.com/Hstarr
Interior Photographs/Illustrations: *AP Photo*: AP Photo (p. 30), Nathan Bilow (p. 25), Bryan Kelsen/Pueblo Chieftain (p. 17), Robert E. Klein (pp. 21, 22, 23), Matt Ryerson/The Hawk Eye (p. 16); Matt Chumley (p. 9); *Getty Images*: Darren England/ALLSPORT (p. 25), Sherman/Hulton Archive (p. 29), Chris Tedesco/Getty Images via Red Bull Photo Files (p. 27); *iStockphoto.com*: ©iStockphoto.com/Hstarr (pp. 5, 8, 19, 20, 27), ©iStockphoto.com/grahamheywood (p. 5); *Shutterstock*: CTR Photos (pp. 7, 19), Glen Gaffney (p. 28), Khafizor Ivan Harisovich (p. 15), Margo Harrison (p. 11), JoLin (p. 13).

Library of Congress Cataloging-in-Publication Data

Tieck, Sarah, 1976-
   Dirt bikes / Sarah Tieck.
      p. cm. -- (Amazing vehicles)
   ISBN 978-1-60453-540-2
   1. Trail bikes--Juvenile literature. I. Title.

TL441.T54 2009
629.227'5--dc22

                                                        2009001755

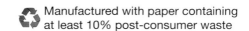
Manufactured with paper containing at least 10% post-consumer waste

CONTENTS

GET MOVING

Imagine you are riding on a dirt bike. Warm air blows past you as you speed along hilly trails. You may even do special **stunts**, such as jumps or spins!

Have you ever looked closely at a dirt bike? Many parts work together to make it move. A dirt bike is an amazing vehicle!

FAST FACT: Dirt bikes that are used for racing are often called motocross bikes.

There are many kinds of dirt bikes. Racing dirt bikes have different colors. These help riders stand out and show off their style.

WHAT IS A DIRT BIKE?

A dirt bike is a type of motorcycle. It is usually ridden off road or on a racetrack.

Its two tires are made to **grip** surfaces. This allows riders to speed through mud, grass, and dirt. Dirt bikes can move quickly and easily over **rugged**, rocky trails.

6

Some people ride dirt bikes for **recreation**, such as outdoor adventures. Others use them for sports, such as racing. Some people even do special tricks and **stunts** on dirt bikes!

Wheelies are one popular trick. To do a wheelie, the driver pops the front wheel off the ground.

A CLOSER LOOK

A dirt bike's body is built on a frame. This frame looks like a motorcycle frame, but it is lighter. It holds the dirt bike's parts together. These parts must be strong enough for racing, jumping, and driving over bumps.

6

1 **Handlebars** help steer a dirt bike. A lever on the handlebars controls the brake. Pulling another lever and twisting the handle helps control the bike's speed.

2 Dirt bike drivers balance on the **seat**. They shift their weight when turning and doing other moves.

3 **Wires** connect the bike's handlebar controls with its moving parts.

4 A dirt bike has a gasoline **engine**.

5 A **kickstand** supports the bike when it's not being ridden.

6 Dirt bike **tires** are similar to bicycle tires. But, they are wider and stronger.

HOW DOES IT MOVE?

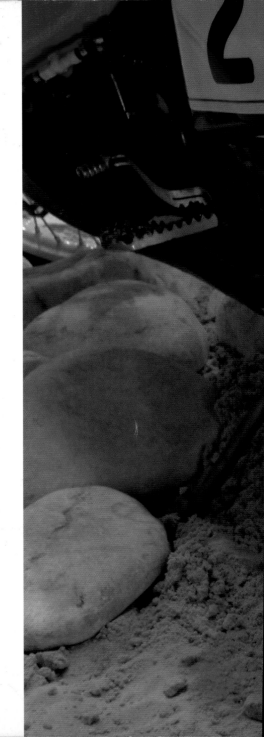

A dirt bike moves when its two wheels turn. But, the wheels need power to move!

The dirt bike's engine supplies that power. It provides enough force to turn an **axle**. This axle is connected to the bike's back wheel. When it turns, the wheels turn.

A dirt bike can move in different directions. The driver uses the handlebars to **steer** it.

The rounded shape of dirt bike tires allows drivers to turn sharply. The outer layer of the tire is called the tread. The pattern in the thick tread keeps the tire from slipping.

POWERFUL ENGINES

Dirt bikes are made to move fast. Because of this, they have powerful engines. An engine's power can be measured in cubic centimeters (ccs). Most dirt bike engines measure between 125 and 500 ccs. More ccs means more power.

Dirt bike engines are built into the bike's frame. Usually, the engine is located between the driver's legs.

THE DRIVER'S SEAT

Dirt bikes are fun and exciting to drive! But, they can also be unsafe. Riders may get hurt. It takes practice and skill to drive them safely.

These machines offer little **protection** for the driver. So, drivers wear protective gear to keep safe. They wear helmets, goggles, gloves, and boots that cover their ankles. Drivers also wear long-sleeved shirts and pants. Many people take special safety classes, too.

Dirt bikes can be ridden by people young and old. Many young riders use minibikes. Some ride for recreation, while others race.

Some dirt bike drivers wear special clothing that is padded. This provides extra protection in case of a fall.

SPEED RACERS

Some dirt bike riders **compete** in motocross races. These races take place all over the world. Winners often receive a cash award.

At motocross events, drivers race at high speeds around dirt or mud tracks. They jump over hills and bumps. Sometimes, they spray dirt as they slide their tires.

Motocross racetracks are carefully designed. They have challenging paths and jumps for racers.

FAST FACT: Motocross racing started in 1924 in Great Britain. It began as off-road racing competitions called scrambles.

STUNTS AND TRICKS

Another form of dirt bike **competition** is Freestyle Motocross (FMX). FMX riders do **stunts** and tricks with their dirt bikes. They do high jumps, backflips, and one-handed moves. Some even make up their own special tricks!

Rider Derek Burlew won an FMX event by doing a Lazy Boy. This trick was invented by rider Travis Pastrana.

FMX riders do tricks on hills or **ramps**. They **compete** at events such as the X Games. They win awards and set records for difficult **stunts** and fast moves.

FMX riders must practice to learn stunts and tricks. They must also practice driving dirt bikes safely at high speeds. Sometimes riders get hurt. But, they can wear **protective** clothes, neck braces, and elbow and knee pads.

st Trick is an FMX event. For this event, riders do one big, ifficult jump for judges. Freestyle is another FMX event. uring Freestyle, riders do a variety of jumps and tricks.

DAREDEVIL RIDERS

For many years, people thought a backflip on a dirt bike was impossible. But at the 2000 Gravity Games, FMX rider Carey Hart did it!

Hart crashed as he landed. So, some people say it was just an attempt. Either way, the event made Hart very famous. It was even featured on the television show *Ripley's Believe It or Not!* Some people call this trick the Hart Breaker.

Carey Hart (*left*) is known for another trick called the Hart Attack. Other types of riders have followed. Now, even snowmobilers (*below*) are doing this trick!

25

Soon, many other dirt bike riders decided to learn **challenging** jumps. By 2007, rider Scott Murray was doing double backflips!

At the 2008 X Games, rider Jim DeChamp attempted a front flip. But, he didn't successfully complete the trick during **competition**.

Foam landing pits helped make these **stunts** possible. Riders can practice jumps in them. If they fall, there is a soft landing space.

At competitions, there are no foam landing pits. So, riders sometimes get hurt doing tricks.

Red Bull X-Fighters is a well-known FMX event. Other well-known events are the X Games and the Gravity Games.

PAST TO PRESENT

In the 1900s, bicycles with motors began to appear. In the 1920s, the first races took place. These early racing motorcycles became popular in the 1950s. Later on, they were called dirt bikes.

Today, some people ride these powerful vehicles on roads and trails. But, mostly they are used in **competitions**. Riders speed around racetracks and perform **stunts**. Dirt bikes are amazing vehicles!

Today's dirt bikes perform much differently from original racing motorcycles. Technology has improved bike design and power.

BLAST FROM THE PAST

Evel Knievel was a famous motorcycle rider. People called him a daredevil for his daring motorcycle **stunts**. Between 1966 and 1981, Knievel did many jumps!

Knievel inspired dirt bike riders, including his son Robbie. When Robbie was eight, he started performing with his father. Today, Robbie often attempts to beat his father's jumping records.

IMPORTANT WORDS

axle (AK-suhl) a bar on which a wheel or a pair of wheels turns.

challenging (CHA-luhn-jihng) testing one's strengths or abilities.

competition (kahm-puh-TIH-shuhn) a contest between two or more persons or groups. To compete is to take part in a competition.

grip to hold tightly.

protect (pruh-TEHKT) to guard against harm or danger. Something that is protective provides protection.

ramp a sloping surface.

recreation (reh-kree-AY-shuhn) an activity done in free time for fun or enjoyment.

rugged having an uneven surface.

steer to guide or control a moving vehicle.

stunt an action requiring great skill or daring.

WEB SITES

To learn more about dirt bikes, visit ABDO Publishing Company online. Web sites about dirt bikes are featured on our Book Links page. These links are routinely monitored and updated to provide the most current information available.

www.abdopublishing.com

INDEX

JAN 1 8			